WHAT DOES A
SMALL FORWARD
DO?

Paul Challen

PowerKiDS
press.

New York

Published in 2017 by The Rosen Publishing Group, Inc.
29 East 21st Street, New York, NY 10010

Developed and Produced for Rosen by BlueApple*Works* Inc.
Managing Editor for BlueApple*Works*: Melissa McClellan
Art Director: Tibor Choleva
Designer: Joshua Avramson
Photo Research: Jane Reid
Editor: Kelly Spence

Basketball is a fluid game; care was taken and every effort was made to portray players in
the identified positions to highlight the content being featured.

Photo Credits: Title page, page borders michelaubryphoto/Shutterstock; title page, p. 6, 8, 9, 16, 17, 18, 19, 22, 23 Aspenphoto/
Shutterstock.com; page backgrounds Eugene Sergeev/Shutterstock; TOC Aleksandar Grozdanovski/Shutterstock; p. 4 T.J. Choleva
/EKS/Shutterstock; p. 5 Eric Broder Van Dyke/Dreamstime.com; p. 7 Keeton Gale/Shutterstock.com; p. 10 Neon Tommy/Creative
Commons; p. 11 Louis Horch/Dreamstime.com; p. 12 joshuak8/Creative Commons; p. 13 Monkey Business Images/Shutterstock;
p. 14 Richard Paul Kane/Shutterstock.com; p. 15, 26 right Keith Allison/Creative Commons; p. 20 Albo/Dreamstime.com; p. 21
Gary Denham/Creative Commons; p. 23 top, 27 top Jerry Coli/Dreamstime.com; p. 24 Stefan Holm/Shutterstock.com; p. 25
skynesher/iStockphoto; p. 26 left Stephen Lew/Keystone Press; p. 27 left Wanghanan/Dreamstime.com; p. 27 right Daniel Raustadt/
Dreamstime.com; p. 28 SpeedKingz/Shutterstock; p. 29 Jamie Roach/Shutterstock.com

Cataloging-in-Publication Data
Names: Challen, Paul.
Title: What does a small forward do? / Paul Challen.
Description: New York : PowerKids Press, 2017. | Series: Basketball smarts | Includes index.
Identifiers: ISBN 9781508151562 (pbk.) | ISBN 9781508150480 (library bound) |
    ISBN 9781508150367 (6 pack)
Subjects: LCSH: Forwards (Basketball)--Juvenile literature. | Basketball--Offense--
    Juvenile literature.
Classification: LCC GV885.C53 2017 | DDC 796.323--dc23

Manufactured in the United States of America
CPSIA Compliance Information: Batch #BS16PK For Further Information contact: Rosen Publishing, New York, New York at 1-800-237-9932

CONTENTS

THE BASKETBALL TEAM

Everyone on a basketball team has an important job to do. On the court, there are five positions: point guard, shooting guard, small forward, power forward, and center. Teammates work together on **offense** to score points, and on **defense** to stop the other team from sinking baskets. All good basketball teams train hard to balance both parts of the game. Coaches teach players the skills they need to be good all-around players.

Each position is assigned a number. This diagram shows where each player is typically positioned when the team is trying to score.

1. Point guard: *The player who is responsible for leading the team and creating scoring opportunities.*

2. Shooting guard: *A player who focuses on scoring baskets, often from a* **wing***, or side, position.*

3. Small forward: *A speedy, skilled player who can score baskets.*

4. Power forward: *A player who uses his or her size to play close to the basket to* **rebound** *and defend.*

5. Center: *Usually the tallest player on the team, the center plays near the net and shoots, rebounds, and blocks shots.*

On offense, teammates **dribble**, **pass**, and shoot to score baskets. On defense, a team works together to stop the other team from scoring and to gain control of the ball. Basketball fans know that the most exciting games are the ones in which both teams battle hard for the ball. It takes lots of practice, teamwork, and communication to prepare a good offense and strong defense for game day.

*The small forward (marked throughout the book with a yellow arrow), along with the power forward and the center, are part of the **frontcourt** on a basketball team. These three players typically play farther forward on the court, inside the three-point line.*

THE SMALL FORWARD

The small forward plays in the frontcourt of a basketball team along with the power forward and the center. As the name suggests, the small forward is usually the smallest of these three players. The player in this position must be a solid all-around player with an excellent ability to pass, score, rebound, and defend. Small forwards combine strength with speed and are always thinking of their next move on the court.

*The small forward might not be the tallest player on the court, but they are often one of the fastest. They use their speed and stamina to play all over the court, both inside and outside the **key**.*

The small forward usually plays around the **perimeter**, between the three-point arc and the key. Sometimes they play inside the key to score baskets from up close. Because a small forward must run back and forth across the court, this player is often also called the "swing man." Defensively, small forwards usually protect the perimeter of the court, but are often called on to defend close to the basket as well.

Small forwards tend to be very versatile players who have a wide range of skills. But every small forward usually has one particular specialty that sets them apart. They might be very accurate shooters, great defensive players, or amazing at picking up rebounds.

OFFENSIVE STRATEGY

On offense, players work together to break down the opposing team's defense. The small forward is often a team's top go-to option for scoring points. Many coaches design special plays to feed the ball to the small forward in different spots on the court. This gives the player in this position a chance to use his or her wide range of shots to put the ball in the basket.

A skilled small forward can sink baskets from all over the court. Each game, the player in this position is often one of the top scorers.

Unlike most of the other positions, the small forward usually has three main tools to score. This player's "triple threat" offense can involve precision shooting from outside the key, dribbling and driving to the basket, or **posting up** defenders near the rim for close-range shots. With such a wide skill set, small forwards are often the top scorers on their team—and in the entire league.

A small forward must pay attention to where their teammates are on the court. It is important to know what other options are available if the shot they are taking could be blocked.

DEFENSIVE STRATEGY

Although players in the small forward position focus much of their efforts on offense, they are also needed on defense. A team will never be successful on the court if one of its five players cannot stop an opponent. At all levels of play, the small forward has to devote a lot of energy and practice to the defensive side of the game.

On defense, small forwards can usually be found trying to stop perimeter shots. But because of their all-around skills, it's not unheard of for a small forward to be able to guard every position!

In the same way that small forwards need to be versatile enough to have a number of offensive weapons, they must also be able to mix it up on defense. Coaches will often ask small forwards to cover both big and small players on defense, meaning they need a combination of speed and strength to do the job. Quick feet, fast hands, and smart positioning to stand up to opponents under the basket are all key.

Covering players of all sizes, small forwards need to be both fast and strong. As a result, small forwards are usually in very good shape.

BALL-HANDLING SKILLS

Although the main responsibility for ball-handling usually falls to the point guard and shooting guard, the small forward still plays an important role in this part of the game. This player has to be skilled in dribbling, able to drive past an opponent at top speed using both hands. Small forwards also need to understand when it is best to dribble while standing still to let the offense get organized for a set play.

The crossover dribble is a popular technique to get past guards. A small forward with the ball will dribble with one hand, and fake going in one direction. When the defender is fooled, the small forward will quickly switch the dribble to his other hand and drive past.

Some small forwards are so good at ball-handling they are known as "point forwards"—a combination of the point guard and forward positions. This gives a team an advantage by being able to start offensive plays from more than one player. Many coaches will also set up plays that move all the offensive players away from the small forward. This gives the small forward the opportunity to play one-on-one against a defender.

Solid ball-handling is an important skill for small forwards to have. It gives them the ability to confidently move the ball all over the court to set up for different scoring opportunities.

13

PASSING THE BALL

To be an effective team player, small forwards need to be good passers. Since they play in the perimeter, the small forward is often in a good position to feed the ball to the center or power forward in the key. If a play needs to be reset, they can swing the ball back out to one of the guards. Small forwards also need to know how to use passing and off-the-ball movement as a way to get open for a shot.

When a small forward receives a pass, they can decide whether to shoot or pass the ball to a teammate who is in a better position to score. Fast hands can be used to snap the ball to another player.

One of the basic passes a small forward needs to master is the chest pass. As its name suggests, this pass is made by holding the ball with both hands at chest level. The player then pushes their arms forward and snaps the ball to a teammate. Another basic pass is the bounce pass, in which a player delivers the ball to a teammate by bouncing it off the court into his or her hands. Fancier, more complicated passes are the behind-the-back and baseball pass.

A small forward who is a good passer often earns a high number of assists. An assist is when a player passes the ball, and the teammate they pass to quickly scores a basket.

SHOOTING THE BALL

There are many types of shots in basketball, and the small forward needs to be skilled at all of them. They require balance, control, and a practiced "shooter's eye." These skills are developed by hours of practice and repetition in the gym, on the playground, or in the driveway. Skilled small forwards recognize when it is best to take a long-range outside shot, or when it is better to drive closer to the basket.

*As well as being able to play near the **post**, a small forward should have a good **jump shot**, and be able to make consistent **three-point shots**.*

Most high-scoring small forwards are able to drive to the basket for spectacular **dunks**—using their speed off the dribble to explode into the air and slam the ball through the hoop. But once in the lane, small forwards also need to know when to change gears and to take more straightforward shots like close-range jump shots, **layups**, or soft "runners," also known as "teardrops" because of their high arc.

There are few things fans love to see more than an awesome slam dunk! It's such a popular move that there's an entire competition dedicated to dunking during the All-Star weekend!

MID-RANGE JUMP SHOT

Small forwards are always on the go, moving into different positions to take shots from all over the court. Because of the way many teams set up their defenses, this player often has an opening to score on a mid-range jump shot. Taken from 10 to 20 feet (3 m to 6.1 m) away from the basket, the small forward dribbles to a spot on the court, then "stops and pops" by jumping up off two feet and shooting the ball from above their head.

A solid jump shot can be one of the most lethal weapons a small forward has. By bending their knees and leaping high into the air above their defender, they can have a clear shot on net.

Many small forwards are also skilled at three-point shooting. Like the mid-range jumper, the small forward can set up for this shot off the dribble, or by running to an open spot on the floor for a **catch-and-shoot** opportunity. Small forwards can set up both mid- and long-range shots by using a teammate as a **screen**.

In the NBA, the three-point arc is 23 feet, 9 inches (7.24 m) away from the basket, except in the corners, where it is 22 feet (6.7 m) away. This means that anyone who is able to consistently hit "treys," or three-pointers, is an incredibly accurate shooter.

GETTING TO THE LINE

The small forward's constant movement and regular attempts at scoring mean that they are typically **fouled** many times per game. That means that anyone playing this position can add to their individual and team point totals by being skilled at making **free throws**. In fact, a look at the scoring tallies of many high-scoring small forwards in any league will reveal that they record a large portion of their points from free throws.

While the small forward makes shots from the free-throw line, their teammates and opponents line up on the other side of the key to prepare for the rebound.

DID YOU KNOW?

One of the NBA's all-time greatest free-throw shooters was Rick Barry. He played in the league (and in the ABA, a rival league) from 1965–1980. Barry once made 21 out of 22 free throws in a game. In another, he shot a perfect 18 for 18. The amazing thing about Barry's skill from the line was that for a large part of his career, he shot free throws "granny style," using an old-school, underhanded technique.

After the **referee** awards a free throw, the shooter gets one, two, or three shots at the basket from the free-throw line. In the NBA, this line is 15 feet (4.6 m) from the basket. Even though opponents are not allowed to block the shot, a free throw can be tough to make when the fans are yelling and everyone's eyes are on the shooter.

Each player has their own approach to free throws. Some players dribble the ball first, while others do not. Consistency is one of the most important parts to sinking a free throw.

UNDER THE RIM

While small forwards are often known for their ability to face up to the basket and shoot from mid and long range, they also need to bring power to their game closer to the basket. That means that they also need to be comfortable playing with their backs to the net, and able to turn and shoot up close. Small forwards need to post up defenders—turning their backs to them to receive the ball with the defender directly behind.

A small forward must be able to hold their ground while posting up. Defenders will try to push them around, and the small forward must stand firm to fight for position.

NBA small forwards have had some amazing nicknames. Paul Pierce of the Los Angeles Clippers, still going strong even though he joined the league in 1998, is known as "The Truth" for his amazing skill and determination on both offense and defense. Julius Erving, one of the first players to master the dunk during his years with the Philadelphia 76ers, was known as "Dr. J." Probably the best nickname among small forwards was the exciting Dominique Wilkins, who played in the NBA from 1982 to 1999. Because of his high-flying offensive moves, Wilkins was called "The Human Highlight Film."

Once the small forward receives the ball, he or she must decide how to turn and shoot. One option is to spin and jump straight up at the defensive player, in an attempt to shoot over the top of the defender's outstretched arms. Another choice is to jump and "fade" backward while shooting. This is a tough shot but gives the shooter some extra room, and is also very hard to block.

Playing close to the post involves all of a small forward's many skills. Not only do they have to stand their ground, they have to be able to spin and shoot very quickly once they receive the ball.

THE ROLE OF A COACH

Many basketball experts say that "practice makes perfect" because of the amount of time it takes to master and perfect basic skills. A good coach is essential for helping players learn and refine the right techniques for shooting, passing, dribbling, rebounding, and defending. Coaches also must make sure players bring those individual skills to each game, blending the strengths of each player and position into a solid and effective team effort.

Every coach is different, and has a different approach to the sport. Some coaches might emphasize offense, while others are more interested in playing a defensive game. But one thing they all have in common is a desire to help each of their athletes play to the best of their abilities.

Coaches also get their teams ready to play in games by inspiring and motivating them. Coaches also give advice to players about the game off the court, providing tips on the importance of a healthy diet, rest, and recovery. Anyone who watches and plays organized basketball for even a short time will see that behind any successful player and team, there is almost always a dedicated coach.

During a time-out, a coach might discuss what the team could do to improve their strategies on offense and defense, go over a specific play, or just offer encouragement.

THE BEST SMALL FORWARDS

There have been hundreds of great small forwards, and basketball fans love to debate who the best all-time players in this position have been. Early greats in this position include John Havlicek, Elgin Baylor, Julius Erving, and Scottie Pippen.

Small forward Kawhi Leonard (left) won an NBA championship with the San Antonio Spurs in 2014 and was named MVP of the NBA Finals. The following year, he was named the league's Defensive Player of the Year.

Kevin Durant (right) of the Oklahoma City Thunder is another current outstanding small forward. His impressive scoring ability has made him the NBA's top scorer four times.

Many basketball fans believe the greatest all-time small forward was Larry Bird. He played his entire NBA career with the Boston Celtics from 1979 to 1992. He later coached the league's Indiana Pacers. Bird wasn't a high flyer like other superstar players—but appearances can be deceiving. Fans loved watching him play with his amazing range of daredevil shots and passes.

Among current players, small forward LeBron James of the Cleveland Cavaliers is considered to be one of the sport's greatest players. James is a four-time league MVP, and won two NBA titles with the Miami Heat in 2012 and 2013. He combines size, speed, and strength and has an unbelievable set of offensive moves in his game.

On the women's side, Maya Moore is one of the game's best small forwards. During her rookie season in 2011–12, Moore helped lead the Minnesota Lynx to a WNBA championship. In 2014, she was named the league MVP.

BE A GOOD SPORT

Good sportsmanship is vital to basketball. Playing to win is a big part of the game, and it can be easy to lose your cool on the court. It is important to remember to show respect for your teammates, opponents, referees, and fans. Making sure that everyone is a good sport also makes the game a lot more fun. Basketball is a great sport for learning to work together as a team to reach a common goal.

Although every player has to develop the individual skills that their position needs, it is equally important to learn teamwork and to approach the game with a positive attitude.

Because small forwards enjoy so much ball possession and are often top scorers, players in this position play an important role in making sure their teammates practice good sportsmanship. With the responsibility for scoring on their shoulders, they can set an example in practice and in games so that everyone stays safe and has fun.

Great small forwards are good team players. They understand that their skills are just one part of what makes a team successful, and that every player on the team needs to work together to win games.

GLOSSARY

assists Plays by one teammate that help others to score.

catch-and-shoot A key offensive skill for a small forward, accomplished by running to an open spot, then receiving a pass from a teammate and shooting, seemingly all in one motion.

defense When a team tries to stop the team with the ball from scoring.

dribble To move the ball up the court by bouncing it with one hand at a time.

dunks Close-range shots executed by jumping up and slamming the ball through the hoop.

fouled When an infraction of the rules of basketball, as determined by the referee in an official game, is called.

free throws Uncontested shots taken from the free throw line that have been awarded after a foul.

frontcourt Where the center, small forward, and power forward play.

jump shot An offensive shot taken by jumping off two feet and releasing the ball at the top of the jump.

key The area of a basketball court that is closest to the basket and marked off by a rectangle with a jump-ball circle at its top.

layups Moving shots, taken by a player who dribbles, takes two quick steps while carrying the ball, and then shoots.

offense When a team has possession of the ball and is trying to score.

pass To throw the ball through the air to a teammate.

perimeter The area of the court located between the key and the three-point line.

post The area on a basketball court located between the basket and the free-throw line.

posting up An offensive move that sees a player position themselves between the ball and a defender, with their back to the basket.

rebound To catch the ball after it bounces off the rim or backboard.

referee The person who enforces the on-court rules of a basketball game.

screen An offensive move in which one player blocks a defender so another teammate can move past.

steals When a player takes the ball from another player.

three-point shots Long-range shots worth three points, taken from behind an arc on the court.

wing In basketball, one of the two sides of the court.

FOR MORE INFORMATION

FURTHER READING

Doeden, Matt. *Basketball Legends in the Making*.
   Mankato, MN: Capstone, 2014.

Gagne, Tammy. *Day by Day with Elena Delle Donne*. Mitchell Lane, 2014.

Garrison, Tarrence. *Basketball Essentials*. Raleigh, NC: Lulu Press, 2014.

Savage, Jeff. *LeBron James*. Minneapolis, MN: Lerner Classroom, 2016.

WEBSITES

Due to the changing nature of Internet links, PowerKids Press has developed an online list of websites related to the subject of this book. This site is updated regularly. Please use this link to access the list:

www.powerkidslinks.com/bs/sforward

INDEX